GOOD FOR ME!

GOOD FOR ME!

Michael's Mom and Dad
(Doctors Nancy & John McNeeley)

publishers since 1798

THOMAS NELSON
PUBLISHERS
Nashville

Dear Parents,

It's not easy! Changes in the world around us have made it more difficult than ever to prepare our children to be the responsible, caring, and productive people we want them to be. Often our children are bombarded with messages which suggest that being bad and doing the wrong thing are more fun than being good. And when our children are away from us and in the company of those who do not share our beliefs, we wish for them to have the strength to always choose to do the right thing.

As parents and psychologists, our work in the ecumenical Christian ministry has guided us as we have developed what we believe to be an exciting way to teach our children the enduring values central to our faith. **Good for Me!** *was written for our son, Michael, and for other early elementary school-aged children.*

The classroom edition of **Good for Me!** *has been used in many Florida elementary schools since 1988 and has been a part of the curriculum of pre-kindergarten programs recognized by the State of Florida as "exemplary." This edition for parents has been modified somewhat to include a more explicit statement of our values, and you will find room in each lesson to share your own beliefs with your child.*

Talented cartoonist, Ken Mitchroney, who works on projects such as **"Teenage Mutant Ninja Turtles,"** *and* **"Tiny Toons,"** *provided the wonderful illustrations and brought our characters to life. We hope you and your child find the program enjoyable and useful.*

Nancy and John McNeeley

For Michael

CONTENTS

INTRODUCTION

JOIN THE CLUB

    We meet four puppies as they set
    goals of Looking Good, Being Good,
    Feeling Good, and Doing Good.

DUSTY LEARNS TO LOOK GOOD

"I'm Somebody Special!"   27

Dusty learns the wellness concepts of good nutrition, exercise, and limited television viewing after exploring the wonders of his senses.

"What Do I See When I Look at Me?"   33

Dusty learns that it is important to look neat and clean, and that a mirror can help!

"My Nose Feels a Tickle!"   39

Dusty learns about germs: how they can make him sick, how they are spread, and what kills them. He learns how important it is to wash his hands regularly!

BOUNCER LEARNS TO BE GOOD

"Sometimes I'm Feeling Bouncy"   47

Bouncer learns that he has more energy than others, and that he sometimes gets in trouble because he has difficulty controlling it. Bouncer

learns self-calming skills which help
him manage his energy.

SNUGGLES LEARNS TO FEEL GOOD

SPOT LEARNS TO DO GOOD

THE PUPPIES SAY, "GOOD-BYE!"

FOREWORD

My list of "things to do today" might look like yours:

—take two children to the orthodontist

—wash Matthew's baseball uniform for game tonight

—listen to Angela's piano lesson

—take snacks for soccer practice.

There's something else, that isn't on my refrigerator list and might not be on yours, either: share your values. Yet, you and I do this continually, and in many different ways.

When we hug a neighbor who's going through tough times, our child observes, "It's good to care for others."

When we go to church, we say to our child, "God is important."

When we clip coupons, we communicate, "Spend money wisely."

But how will my child—or yours—make the jump from seeing your values, to adopting those behaviors for himself?

With all the changes, stressors, and pressures of the 90's, we can't depend on accidental or incidental teaching of values. We must practice intentional parenting. The stakes are too high; we can't leave value-sharing to chance.

This doesn't need to be tough, boring, or even "heavy." Just ask Michael McNeeley. He's 13 years old now, and he'll be honest with you. His parents Nancy and John McNeeley, wanted to help Michael learn how to act responsibly, deal with stress, and feel proud of himself when he made good choices. So the three McNeeleys sat down and put together a program called "Good for Me." Michael contributed the problems and perspectives of a pre-adolescent. Nancy and John, both clinical psychologists, brought years of training and professional experience.

Good for Me! moved off the McNeeleys kitchen table. It was adopted by school districts. The program won awards. And now, John and Nancy have adapted "Good for Me" for parents to use with their children.

Good for Me! can provide a handle for you and me to give our children the basic tools they need so they'll do the right thing when we're not around . . . when they're in the back seat of a car . . . when they're handed something in front of the lockers at school . . . when someone says, "It's more fun to be bad than to be good."

As an educator, I agree wholeheartedly with the concepts presented in this book. As a parent, I am grateful for the McNeeleys' realistic approach to these vital issues. I sincerely encourage you to apply to your everyday parenting the principles presented in this book.

Good for Me! offers a way to see and hear what our kids are thinking about, what's important to them, and share what's important to us. When we invest time and effort today, our children can more effectively meet the challenges of tomorrow.

—Dr. Mary Manz Simon

INTRODUCTION

- **The Skills and the Teachers**
- **How the Program Works**
- **Special Problems of the '90's**
- **Working with the Program**
- **Other Fun Things to Do**

ABOUT THE PROGRAM

The Skills and the Teachers

Dusty wants to be well-groomed, healthy, and energetic, but he has lots of long hair to manage, he watches too much television, and he eats too much junk food. As Dusty learns that he is special and that he should take better care of himself, he is proud of himself when he can **Look Good.**

I can Look Good!

DUSTY

I can Be Good!

BOUNCER

Bouncer wants to stay out of trouble! But he has lots of energy, and he often does things without thinking. He learns that when he is calm, he finds it easier to follow rules, act responsibly, use good judgment, resolve conflicts without fighting, and finish what he starts. Bouncer learns to calm down, and he is proud of himself when he can **Be Good.**

1

Snuggles wants to bring out the best in himself by developing his special talents and expressing the love he feels. He is a loving puppy who lives in a world that can sometimes be painful. When he feels discouraged or lonely, he learns how to feel better by using his imagination to create a special place where he feels safe and loved. He finds the courage to resist peer pressure, and to look within himself for guidance in making good choices. Snuggles is proud of himself when he can **Feel Good.**

I can Feel Good!

SNUGGLES

I can Do Good!

Spot wants to be a gentler, more considerate puppy. He knows how to be his best self, but he sometimes forgets to use good manners, and sometimes it is hard for him to apologize when he makes mistakes. Spot also learns that we share the earth with all other living things, and he wants to learn how he can take better care of the environment and make our world a better place for all of us. Spot learns to be his very best self, and he is proud of himself when he can **Do Good.**

SPOT

How the Program Works

"Developmental Readiness"

Children between the ages of 4 and 7 are very receptive to learning good—or bad—social skills. During this period of childhood, they are busy trying to figure out how boys and girls are supposed to act. They look carefully at you, other family members, teachers, friends, schoolmates, and characters in books, television programs, and movies as they decide what boys and girls should do, think, and feel.

It is crucial for your child to learn good social skills at an early age because learning them later can really be difficult. And more than ever, your child needs a healthy foundation to build on because of the challenges that lie ahead!

Right and Wrong

Children of this age begin to form a basic "right and wrong" sense of justice and fairness. They respect adults and see them as powerful figures who can give them rewards or punishments. At this age, your child needs very much to please you and other adults, but if this is not possible, your child will seek to please other children. This may or may not be a good thing!

In a world of mixed messages, it's important for you to let your child know what you expect good boys and good girls to do, to freely give approval and disapproval, and to be fair.

3

Rhymes to Remember

We memorized lots of things in elementary school . . . state capitols, world geography, the names of our presidents . . . yet it would be next to impossible for most of us to recall them correctly now. And yet, most of us still remember, *"i before e, except after c . . ."*, a simple rule to use when meeting the challenge of spelling new words. Just as that little rhyming phrase still helps us spell new words, *Good for Me!* gives children rhyming phrases (the most important lines are in bold print) which are intended to help them in real life situations. The first begins,

I am growing! Good for Me!
I can be anything I want to be!

You can't be with your child all the time, but you can give him these messages to remind him to make good decisions and be his very best self!

The Lessons to Be Learned

Because the world responds to us based on how we look and how we act, *Good for Me!* wants to get children off to a good start by first teaching them to **Look Good** and to **Be Good.** When your child makes an effort to stay neat and clean and to follow the rules, the world is a much friendlier and more helpful place!

Once children can **Look Good** and **Be Good,** they are encouraged to **Feel Good** by creatively expressing their special talents and loving feelings. Finally, children learn to **Do Good** by using good manners, taking responsibility for their mistakes, acting to make the world a better place, and being their very best selves. Children who learn these lessons have a real advantage in the world!

4

Special Problems of the '90s

Alcohol and Substance Abuse

There will always be children who try to teach others that being bad is more fun than being good. Children need to choose friends who want to do the right thing, to know how to have fun in creative, healthy ways, and how to "say no" when the time comes.

"Saying No" is presented as something to be proud of when encouraged to do the wrong thing by "friends."

Communicable Diseases

"Good for Me!" teaches children that illnesses are caused by germs, and that germs can be passed to others by dirty hands, through the air, and by contact with body fluids and blood. They learn that soap kills germs, and they are encouraged to wash regularly! Children are also taught that when they are ill, they are expected to take precautions to avoid spreading germs to others. The "common cold" is used as the example; other communicable diseases (such as AIDS) are not specifically mentioned.

Also, children cannot be expected to "say no" to activities that place them at risk for getting the AIDS virus and other communicable diseases without self-discipline and good decision making skills. *Good for Me!* teaches these skills, too!

Working with the Program

Good for Me! contains 16 lessons organized in four major units. The first lesson **("Join the Club!")** introduces the puppies and the program, and a final **"Good-bye"** includes an award for the puppies and for your child.

All the lessons contain:

Parent's Guides   Each Parent's Guide contains the reason for the lesson, suggestions for getting the most from the lesson, and ideas for other fun things to do.

Teaching Talks   The puppies teach each lesson by talking about themselves and the problems they must solve. They ask your child to think about and share experiences and problems, too. (Things to talk about with your child are in bold print.)

Poems   Each poem contains powerful messages about doing the right thing and being your best self. You might wish to encourage your child to memorize the parts of each poem in bold print.

Workbook Pages   The puppies ask your child to draw pictures or write about things they are proud of.

Take your time as you work through the lessons. Talk to each other, learn from each other, and have fun together!

Other Fun Things to Do

Making Puppets   Puppets can add interest to the program, and you could make your own together. (You could use old socks or even paper bags!)

It can be fun to put on puppet shows, and if you have access to a video camera, you could even produce your own television programs!

Other Lessons   The puppies can help you reinforce other lessons you want your child to learn. Call on Dusty to help you talk about good grooming, good health, good food, and limiting TV viewing. Bouncer can be helpful when you discuss the rules at home and at school, safety, and good judgment. Snuggles can help talk about feelings, creative self-expression, and saying no to peer pressure. And Spot can help with good manners, being your best self, and environmental responsibility.

Journals   Finally, you and your child might wish to keep *"Good for Me!"* Journals in which you write about or draw pictures of things you have done during the day to be proud of.

The puppies invite your child to . . .

JOIN THE CLUB!

In the first lesson, we meet the puppies and they invite your child to join their *Good for Me!* Club!

Parent's Guide to . . . JOIN THE CLUB!

The Reason for This Lesson

Right now your child is busy putting together a very special puzzle, and you can help! When he finishes, it will help him decide what to do, what to think, and what to feel about his world. Boys are busy putting together a puzzle in their minds that might be called "the ideal boy," and girls are putting together their idea of "the ideal girl."

Everywhere they look, children find another piece of the puzzle. They watch you and listen to the stories you tell. They watch their teachers and their neighbors. They find more parts as they watch other boys and girls. And they find pieces as they watch television and movies.

As this puzzle takes shape, your child wants very much to be like the picture he is creating. And as long as your child sees lots of good examples of how boys and girls should act and feel, the pieces in the "ideal child" puzzle will be healthy and useful. On the other hand, if your child's puzzle has bad examples of how boys and girls act, you may not be so pleased!

Each *Good for Me!* lesson can be thought of as a separate piece of the "ideal child" puzzle. The first lesson helps you get started by talking about heroes, because heroes have many of the qualities you would want your child to place in his puzzle.

The Story We meet four puppies as they talk about their hero and each shares his reasons for wanting to be like him. They form the *"Good for Me!"* Club and promise do at least one thing each day that they are proud of. Then they invite your child to "Join the Club!"

Getting the Most from This Lesson

Encourage your child to have heroes.

Heroes take good care of themselves, act responsibly, follow rules, and use good judgment. They are courageous and do not yield to temptation to do the wrong thing, and they work to make the world a better place. And they never act like bullies!

Form a *"Good for Me"* Club with your child and start each day with the *"Good for Me!"* Cheer.

Complete the membership certificate on page 20.

Start each day by saying the *Good for Me!* Cheer, and make up your own special signal to be used with a smile that means, "I saw what you did and I am proud of you!" Use it whenever you see your child doing the right thing. It's fun to end each day by sharing good examples of **Looking Good, Being Good, Feeling Good,** or **Doing Good** that you saw during the day. You could make a *"Good for Me!"* Journal, and each day your child can write about or draw pictures of something he is proud of.

Other Fun Things to Do

- Identify heroes in the news every day who are making the world a better place. You could even write to them and send them an honorary membership in your *"Good for Me!"* Club! It's also important to talk about heroic actions of family members, past and present.

- Have a **"Dress as Your Hero Day."** Make costumes and talk about how your child's heroes would act in different situations throughout the day. (You could dress as your hero, too!)

---

*Your child does **lots** of good things every single day! And when he pleases you, be sure to let him know it with lots of smiles and hugs! Your approval is the glue that helps hold his puzzle pieces in place.*

2

The puppies invite your child to . . . # JOIN THE CLUB!

DUSTY

Hi, I'm Dusty, and I want to tell you about our *"Good for Me!"* Club. My friends and I started it because we want to be like our hero, Sparky, the Wonder Dog, because he is always his very best self.

BOUNCER

I'm Bouncer, and I want to do the right thing and be proud of myself, like our hero, Sparky.

I'm Snuggles, and I know that sometimes it's not easy to be your very best self. I'm glad I have good friends to help me.

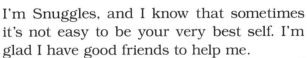

SNUGGLES

SPOT

I'm Spot, and I'm glad to meet you. Our club has helped us learn new ways of being proud of ourselves. We hope that you will join, too!

13

I like being in the *"Good for Me!"* Club be-cause I want to learn to take better care of myself and stay healthy. I want to **Look Good** like Sparky! He is always neat and clean and he always has lots of energy. It takes lots of energy to be a hero!

It is hard for me to look my best all the time because I have so much long hair to take care of. It gets messy and dirty when I play, and I'm learning to wash it every day so that it smells nice and looks neat. And now I wash my hands with soap to kill the germs that can make me sick so that I stay healthy, like Sparky!

My favorite thing to do after school is watch TV and eat junk food, but I'm learning to change all that because I know Sparky wouldn't spend all his time in front of a TV set!

The "Good for Me!" Club helps me feel proud of myself when I Look Good. I hope you join, too!

DUSTY

I like being in the *"Good for Me!"* Club because I want to learn to stay out of trouble! I want to **Be Good** like Sparky! Sparky always follows the rules and he always thinks about what might happen before he does something. And he always tries to solve problems without fighting. He only fights if he has to, and he never acts like a bully!

It is hard for me to stay out of trouble because I have lots of energy, and I do things without thinking first. I know that it is wrong to jump around and push people, and I'm learning to calm down and think about things before I do them. That's what Sparky does!

The "Good for Me!" Club helps me feel proud of myself when I can Be Good. I hope you join, too!

BOUNCER

I like to be in the *"Good for Me!"* Club because I want to learn to be happy, especially when things don't go right for me. I want to **Feel Good** like Sparky! He always looks so happy, and he is good at so many things. I'm learning that I'm good at lots of things, too!

And Sparky never gives up, no matter how hard things are for him. Lots of the people I love live far away from me and I miss them a lot. And sometimes I feel sad and all alone. I'm learning how to send my love to people far away, and I'm learning that there are lots of things I can do to feel better when I am unhappy.

The "Good for Me!" Club helps me feel proud of myself when I Feel Good. I hope you join, too!

SNUGGLES

16

I like being in the *"Good for Me!"* Club because I want to learn to be my very best self. I want to **Do Good** like Sparky! Sometimes I forget to use good manners, and sometimes it is really hard for me to say, "I'm sorry," when I make a mistake.

And I want to learn to care for our world the way that Sparky does. He is always trying to make the world a better place. I'm learning how important it is to recycle our trash, to reuse things instead of throwing them away, and to use only what we need. And I'm learning to care for the other people and animals in the world so that the world is a good place for them to be, too.

The "Good for Me!" Club helps me feel proud of myself when I Do Good. I hope you join, too!

SPOT

In our *"Good for Me!"* Club, we all want to be our very best selves, and we promise to do something to be proud of every day.

We say a special *"Good for Me!"* cheer to help us remember to always Look Good, Be Good, Feel Good, and Do Good. We hope you will learn to say it, too!

We know that being your best self is not always easy, so we have a secret way of helping each other. When we see someone being their very best self, we send them a secret **"thumbs up"** signal that means, "I saw what you did, and I am proud of you!"

If you promise to do something to be proud of every day, you can join our *"Good for Me!"* Club! And when you do something to be proud of, remember to say to yourself, *"Good for Me!"* like we do.

There's a membership certificate for you on page 20!

Good for Me!

I am growing! Good for me!
I can be anything I want to be!

I can **Look Good.**
I can **Be Good.**

I am full of possibilities!

I can **Feel Good.**
I can **Do Good.**

The world is a wonderful place to be!

I am growing! Good for me!
I can be anything I want to be!

This is to certify that

_____

is a member of the
"GOOD FOR ME!"
Club.

The pledge:

As a member of the _"Good for Me!"_ Club, I promise to do something to be proud of every day.

_____
Member's Signature

_____
Witness

_____
Date

Dusty learns about . . .

LOOKING GOOD

"I'M SOMEBODY SPECIAL!"

The Reason for This Lesson

While we all laugh at the "couch potato," we know that this lifestyle can contribute to serious health problems! Right now your child is developing eating habits, exercise habits, and television viewing habits that will either serve him well in his future or will cause problems for him.

About television: We also know that human beings do not like to be bored. Boredom is a most uncomfortable feeling, and many of us automatically turn on the television set to feel better. (Even watching something stupid feels better than being bored!) When we develop this habit, we give up more and more of our ability to define and create our lives, and we learn that unpleasant feelings can be quickly and easily avoided. This habit does not serve our children well when it comes time for them to say no.

And we know that children love to learn, and are **always** learning something! We also need to be aware of what they are learning from the television programs they are watching!

This lesson encourages your child to see himself as "somebody special" who should take good care of himself by eating healthy foods, exercising, getting enough rest at night, and limiting his television viewing. With the TV set off, opportunity abounds for your child to discover lots of healthy and creative things to do!

The Story Dusty almost turns to stone because he has been watching too much TV and eating too much junk food! Then he thinks about all the wonderful things his senses can do, and he decides to take better care of himself so he can continue to enjoy all of life's wonders!

Getting the Most from This Lesson

Talk about your child's favorite sensory experiences and favorite fresh food to eat.

Take a walk with all senses open and draw pictures of favorite things when you're done. Grow your own fresh foods to snack on!

Have a regular bedtime!

All of us need sleep to stay healthy! Talk about how the body works during sleep to repair all the things that need to be fixed, and to help us stay well.

Discover fun things to do instead of watching TV.

Encourage your child to develop interests in things other than TV!

(About video games: Video games are definitely not passive entertainment! Playing can improve short and long term memory, eye-hand coordination, and problem solving ability. And they teach important lessons about dealing with frustration and trying again! But, as with any good thing, moderation is the key!)

Other Fun Things to Do

- Have a family "No TV" night each week. Select one weekday evening when you all agree not to turn on the television set. Do things together, like making seasonal decorations, playing games, or telling stories about family heroes. For more good ideas, your child can ask grandparents and great-grandparents how they spent their time before TV!

When you see your child developing life-style habits that will serve him well, be sure to let him know how proud you are of him!

---

3 "I'M SOMEBODY SPECIAL!"

Dusty learns . . .

I want to tell you about something that happened to me last week. I hope it never happens to you!

I was watching TV and eating cookies and candy and chips and drinking a soda, and guess what happened? All of a sudden I couldn't get up! Lucky for me that my friend, Spot, came over and helped me. He told me that I could turn into a stone statue if I watched any more TV! He took me outside into the fresh air right away, and I felt fine again!

Spot told me that I am somebody special, and I should think about all the things my body does for me. It lets me see beautiful things and hear music and smell flowers and taste pizza and feel hugs.

What special things do you like to see and hear and smell and taste and touch? You're somebody special, too!

DUSTY

I learned that my body needs good food to eat and that fresh food from the earth is better than candy and chips and sodas! Now I eat more fruit and vegetables and drink more juice, and I feel better. **What are your favorite fresh foods to eat?**

And I learned that when I sleep at night, my body grows and fixes the things that need to be fixed. Now I go to bed when I am supposed to so my body can get the rest it needs. **When is your bedtime?**

I also learned that I need exercise and fresh air, too, and that sitting in front of the TV set all the time was not good for me. Now I have lots of fun doing other things! **What do you like to do instead of watching TV?**

I wrote a poem to help me remember how special I am and what I need to do to take good care of me. I hope it helps you remember, too. When you take good care of yourself, be proud of yourself, and say to yourself, **"Good for Me!"**

Draw a picture of things you do to take good care of yourself on page 28. Remember, you're somebody special!

"I'm Somebody Special!"

**I'm Somebody Special! I'm special to me!
Because I'm so special, I take good care of me.**

My eyes can see colors and rainbows above,
And blue skies and sunsets, and faces I love.

My ears can hear music and wonderful sounds
Like bird songs and laughter, and rain falling down.

My nose can smell flowers and bread as it's baked,
And there are good foods that I love to taste.

My body can dance and jump and run.
My skin can feel breezes and tickles and hugs.

**I'm Somebody Special! I'm special to me!
Because I'm so special, I take good care of me.**

The earth around me gives me things that I need
To grow strong and healthy and live happily.

Fresh foods from the earth and clean air to breathe
Are just what I need to take good care of me.

The earth gives me sunshine and places to play,
And in the moonlight, I dream troubles away.

All of these gifts are special to me.
And I enjoy them much more than TV!

**I'm Somebody Special! I'm special to me!
Because I'm so special, I take good care of me.**

This is me taking good care of myself.

Parent's Guide to ... LOOKING GOOD!

The Reason for This Lesson

In the world we live in, neatness does count! When your child goes out into the world, ideally people are helpful to him, patient, and supportive. His chances of getting this kind of help are greater if he is clean and well groomed, and makes an effort to keep himself that way.

And it's important for your child to become more aware of himself. You want him to know when he needs to blow his nose, wash his hands, brush his teeth, comb his hair, zip his zippers, tie his shoes, or wipe peanut butter off his cheek!

Finally, because of the presence of AIDS and other communicable diseases in our world, it is more important than ever for your child to develop the habits of regular hand washing and bathing.

The Story   Dusty has a problem that he must overcome: Because he has so much hair, he has to work extra hard to stay neat and clean. He discovers that a mirror can be a great help!

Getting the Most from This Lesson

Help your child get in the habit of cleaning up during the day each time he needs to.

Make sure that your child has everything he needs to start his day neat and clean: soap for his hands and face, a toothbrush and toothpaste for his smile, a comb or brush for his hair, clean clothes to wear, and a mirror to check his progress!

The best health habit you can teach your child is regular hand washing. Even though it takes some time, he should always wash his hands after using the bathroom and always before eating.

To make sure hands get thoroughly washed, teach him to lather and scrub while he sings a song from start to finish, or while he counts slowly to ten, or while he says the *"Good for Me!"* Cheer! You can use the same technique to make sure he is doing a good job of brushing his teeth! And encourage him to take a bath or shower every day!

Other Fun Things to Do

- To encourage self awareness, it can be fun to make life-sized self portraits! You can tape several grocery bags together to make a big sheet of paper as large as your child. Have him lie down on the paper while you trace around his body. Cut out the tracing and hold it next to him while he looks in a mirror. Help him choose colors that match his eyes and hair. (You could use yarn for hair if you want to get fancy!) For clothing, ask your child to think about his favorite things to wear. Draw and color clothing paying attention to all the buttons, zippers, and laces (or glue on cloth, buttons, or construction paper!). Display his work of art—your child at his best, "Looking Good!"

- A full-length mirror can really help you teach your child to be well groomed. Say the poem together and teach him to scan himself from head to toe to be sure he knows how to "Look Good" on his own.

- Make a grooming kit with your child. Make sure it contains a comb or brush, a nail brush, tissues, and a hand mirror. Empty tissue boxes work well. Decorate them with Dusty's picture if you wish!

Start each day by giving a compliment to your child on his appearance, and be sure to notice when he makes an extra effort to Look Good!

Dusty learns about . . . LOOKING GOOD

Can you guess why people call me Dusty? I was named Dusty because sometimes I look like a dust rag when I play outside! I have got lots and lots and lots of hair, and when I play outside and get hot and sweaty, the dirt sticks to it and I smell bad! I get dirty when I eat, too. Food gets on my face and hands, and I am a mess! But that's not all. My hair even gets messy when I sleep! When I get up in the morning, some of it is matted down, and some of it sticks straight up! **Does that ever happen to you?**

When I was little, someone helped me keep my hair neat and clean, and washed my face and hands, and brushed my hair, and made sure that I took a bath every night so I wouldn't smell bad. And someone always helped me brush my teeth so that they wouldn't hurt or get holes in them. And someone made sure that I had clean clothes to wear every day and helped me get dressed. They even buttoned my buttons for me!

31

Now that I am older, it is up to me to do those things for myself. It's not always easy for me to remember when to brush my hair or wash my face and hands, but I found something to help me. **Can you guess what it is?** It's a mirror! I take a minute before school and after I play and after I eat to look in the mirror and check myself over. Then I know right away what I need to do to look good again! **Do you know how to check yourself from head to toe to be sure that you look good?**

I wrote a poem to help me remember what to look at when I check myself in the mirror. I hope it helps you, too! When you can keep yourself neat and clean from your head to your toes, be proud of yourself and say to yourself, **"Good for Me!"**

> Draw a picture of yourself Looking Good on page 34.

What Do I See
When I Look at Me?

What do I see when I look at me?
From head to toe, I'm as neat as can be!

First I check my hair—
I see it's neat up there!
(It smells good, too!)

Then I check my face—
It's clean, every place!
(Even behind my ears!)

Then I check my teeth—
And see my smile is so sweet!
(I brush my teeth twice a day!)

Then I check my hands—
They're clean and looking so grand!
(Even my fingernails are clean!)

Then I check my clothes—
Up above and down below.
(My buttons are buttoned, and my zippers are zipped!)

Then the last thing to do
Is check the laces in my shoes.
(You won't see me tripping over my shoelaces!)

That's what I see when I look at me!
From head to toe, I'm as neat as can be!
(I'm Looking Good!)

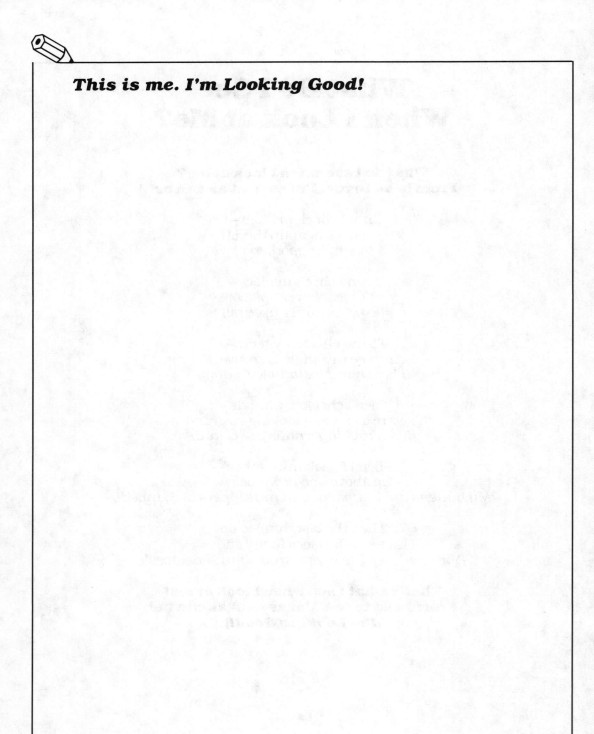

This is me. I'm Looking Good!

STAYING HEALTHY

The Reason for This Lesson

The growing threat of communicable diseases such as AIDS makes it more important than ever for your child to understand how diseases are spread, how to stay healthy, and how to take care of himself when he does get sick. Medical experts continue to believe that the only effective prevention of communicable diseases is through education. It is important for your child to learn that diseases are caused by germs, and that germs can also be spread by contact with infected blood.

Because your child is likely to catch a cold at some time, this lesson teaches that we catch colds by coming into contact with the virus, and then getting the virus into our bodies by breathing it in or by putting dirty hands in and around our mouths. The emphasis is on prevention by regular hand washing to kill germs.

The Story Dusty has caught another cold! He learns that germs cause illnesses, and that soap kills germs. He also learns that some people have germs in their blood. He decides to wash his hands more often!

He also learns that when he is sick he can spread his germs to others by coughing and sneezing into the air, and Dusty wants to be sure that he does not spread his germs to anyone else while he is sick. So he learns to do the right thing by covering his coughs and sneezes and washing his hands.

Getting the Most from This Lesson

Talk about how germs get inside your body.

Dirty hands carry lots of germs into your body! The most important thing you can do for your child is to let him see you wash your hands before meals or snack time. (Keep soapy washcloths and towels in the car to use when you are away from home!)

And when you have to come in contact with blood, let your child see you wash with soap afterward and disinfect any surfaces that the blood has touched.

Talk about how we spread germs when we are sick.

Your child needs a good supply of tissues when he has a cold, a place to dispose of them, and a place to wash his hands! And he needs to cover his coughs and sneezes, too!

Other Fun Things to Do

- If you want to show your child that germs are on everyone's hands, and that soap kills germs, try this! You, too, will be amazed! You will need a potato, a potato peeler, soap, and two closed containers.

  Before washing your hands, cut the potato in half, peel half of it, and put the peeled half in a closed container. Wash your hands and the potato peeler with soap. Peel the other half of the potato and place it in a closed container. Let it stand overnight. Yikes! More germs from dirty hands mean more of a chance to get sick!

  If you want your child to understand how the germs get on people's hands in the first place, peel a potato with clean hands then touch different surfaces around the house and outside (door handles, etc.) with the potato and place it in a closed container. Germs are everywhere!

Be sure to let your child know that your are proud of him when he tries to act responsibly when he is sick. And allow extra time for him to wash his hands during the day. It could help you stay healthy, too!

Dusty talks about . . . # STAYING HEALTHY

Have you ever been sick? I had a cold last week, and I was sick! I feel better now, but I decided to learn about what made me sick so I that I won't get sick again soon! **Do you know what makes you sick?** Germs! Germs make you sick. They are little teeny tiny things that you can't even see, but if they get inside your body, they can make you sick. **Do you know how germs get inside your body?** You breathe the germs into your body through your nose or mouth, or if your hands are dirty and you put them into your mouth, or near your mouth, the germs can get inside your body that way. Sometimes people who are sick have germs in their blood, and if the germs in their blood get inside your body, you can get sick, too.

I heard that there are ways that you can kill germs before they can make you sick!

Do you know how to kill germs before they can make you sick?

You can use soap! Soap kills germs before they can make you sick. You should **always** wash your hands with soap after you use the bathroom and before you eat if you want to stay healthy!

Sometimes you get sick anyway, even when you try your best to stay healthy. And when you are sick, it's your job to be sure that you don't spread germs to other people. **Do you know how you spread germs to other people when you are sick?** Germs leave your body through your nose and mouth when you sneeze or cough, so you should cover your sneezes and coughs, take care of your runny nose, and wash the germs off your hands with soap when you are done.

I wrote a poem to help me remember how to keep from spreading germs when I am sick. When you know how to stay healthy and how to keep from spreading germs when you are sick, be proud of yourself, and say to yourself, **"Good for Me!"**

Draw a picture of soap killing germs on page 40.

38

My Nose Feels a Tickle!

My nose feels a tickle!
I am going to sneeze!

Uh, oh!
Look out!
Here it comes!
Pass the tissues, please!

Uh, oh! My nose is running!
I'll catch it right away!
I'll blow it in a tissue,
Then I'll go back to play.

Uh, oh! My throat is tickly!
A cough is on its way.
I'll cover up my mouth real fast
Until it goes away.

Uh, oh! My hands are dirty!
They'll never do this way!
Where's the soap and water?
I need it right away!

This is soap.

These are germs.

This is soap killing germs.

Bouncer learns about . . .

BEING GOOD

Parent's Guide to . . . CALMING DOWN

The Reason for This Lesson

Children are truly blessed with an amazing amount of energy and enthusiasm! Even an Olympic athlete would have trouble keeping up with them! Some children seem to have been "blessed" more than others, and it can be a special challenge to parents to keep up with them. Some children would challenge the entire Olympic team!

Children with lots of energy can find themselves in trouble a lot, and even in dangerous situations, because they may not be very good at slowing down and thinking before they act. And we find ourselves saying, "Slow down!" or "Calm down!" a lot.

This lesson helps you teach your child how to calm down by using a special breathing technique ("Bouncer Breathing"). When our breathing is slow and controlled, our bodies are controlled and we can more easily calm down and think before we act.

If your child is blessed with more than his share of energy, he needs to meet Bouncer and learn "Bouncer Breathing!"

The Story   Bouncer talks about how his "bouncy" times often lead to problems in school and with friends. He has trouble getting his work done, he talks out in class, and he has trouble staying in line. He learns a special breathing technique that he calls his "Bouncer Breathing" to help him calm down and stay out of trouble!

43

Getting the Most from This Lesson

Talk about the times when your child has trouble calming down.

Some children with lots of energy are fine when they are at home or when they are just with a few other people, but when they are in places where there's lots going on, they tend to get into trouble and their energy gets the best of them. Noisy, crowded places like malls, supermarkets, or restaurants can be particularly challenging! Certain times at school (like walking in line or playing at recess can also be difficult times for self control.

Teach your child to use "Bouncer Breathing" when it's time to calm down.

Here's how to breathe like Bouncer: First, take a slow, deep breath in through your nose, hold the breath while counting slowly to three, and then blow all the air out slowly and softly through your mouth. When doing "Bouncer Breathing," focus your attention on something that is always with you, like a certain finger, or a special place on your wrist. You may need to close your eyes while calming down, and you may need to repeat the "Bouncer Breathing" several times!

Other Fun Things to Do

- If your child has lots of energy and needs to calm down regularly, make a special bracelet to help focus attention while doing "Bouncer Breathing." You can point to it as a special signal to calm down when you are away from home.

When you see your child trying to calm down, be sure to let him know you are proud of him! (You can use "Bouncer Breathing," too! It's really helpful when you are nervous or when you are trying to get to sleep!)

Bouncer talks about . . . CALMING DOWN

Can you guess why people call me Bouncer? People call me Bouncer because I have **lots** of energy, and sometimes I run around so much that I look like a bouncing ball! Sometimes bouncing gets me in trouble in school because I talk out in class and I don't get my work done. When I am bouncy, it is hard for me to stay in my place in line. And sometimes it is hard for me to take turns when I play with my friends. And people are always saying, "You need to calm down!" Bouncing gets me in trouble at home, too!

Does bouncing ever get you in trouble?

Well, I learned that I can't be bouncy and calm at the same time, and that when my breathing is slow and calm, my whole body is calm. And when I am calm, it's easier to pay attention, concentrate, get my work done, and stay out of trouble, too! Here's what I do when I need to calm down.

First, I talk to myself and tell myself, "I need to calm down right now. I can do it!" Then I find something still to look at. I like to look at a special spot on my desk at school.

Then I take a big, deep breath slowly through my nose. I hold my breath while I count slowly to myself, "One . . . Two . . . Three."

Then I let my breath out slowly through my mouth and it makes a whispering sound like, *"Whoooooosh,"* as all the air goes out.

If I'm still not calm, I do it again until my mind and body are calm. Sometimes I need to close my eyes when I calm down.

I've written a poem to help me remember how important it is to calm down. I hope it helps you, too. When you have learned how to calm yourself down, be proud of yourself, and say to yourself, **"Good for Me!"**

Draw a picture of yourself doing your "Bouncer Breathing" on page 48.

46

Sometimes I'm Feeling Bouncy

Sometimes I'm feeling bouncy
And jittery inside.
I want to jump and run around,
But it's not the right time!

So I calm down and take a breath
As big as I can take,
And hold it while I count to three,
Then I let it out this way:
"Whoooooosh"

And then I'm feeling better
And much more in control.
And I stay out of trouble
When I am calm, you know!

Sometimes when I am bouncy
And running all around,
That's the time when things go wrong.
I hit or scream or shout.

So I calm down and take a breath
As big as I can take,
And hold it while I count to three,
Then I let it out this way:
"Whoooooosh"

And then I'm feeling better
And much more in control.
And I stay out of trouble
When I am calm, you know!

This is me calming down.

GROWING UP

The Reason for This Lesson

We are **all** growing! The good news is that as we grow, we gain competence in the world and can make lots more choices about our lives. The bad news is that we work harder and more is expected of us! As he grows, your child will be expected to follow more rules and take more responsibility at home and at school. But there will be more things for him to enjoy and be proud of, like riding a two-wheeler and learning to read and playing video games. What thrills!

The Story   Bouncer discovers that some of his clothes are too small for him now and that "he's not as young as he used to be!" He is proud of himself when he learns to take care of his chores and follow the rules at home and at school.

Getting the Most from This Lesson

Your child does lots of fun things now that he couldn't do when he was little.

Children love to hear stories about the things they did when they were babies and toddlers! Look at baby pictures and talk about what your child liked to do when he was little. Talk about how much he has grown and how much he has learned to do since then!

What are your child's responsibilities at home? What chores does he do?

Children feel proud of themselves when they take part in household chores and take care of their responsibilities! The important thing to remember is to give your child responsibilities around the house that he can successfully handle, and be sure to conduct several "on the job" training sessions so that he will know what is expected of him.

What are the rules and responsibilities at school?

Talk to your child's teacher about the rules at school and let your child know that you are proud of him when he follows the rules!

Other Fun Things to Do

- Make a grow chart and hang it on the wall to keep track of your child's height. You could even put the *"Good for Me!"* cheer on it ("I am growing! Good for Me! I can be anything I want to be!" . . .).

- Look through your child's old clothes together. He is growing!

Let your child know how proud you are of him when he does his chores and follows the rules!

Bouncer talks about . . . GROWING UP

Guess what has been happening to me! My clothes are shrinking! My favorite clothes keep getting smaller and smaller and smaller, and now they don't fit me anymore! **Has that ever happened to you?**

People tell me that my clothes don't fit because I have grown too big for them! And there are lots of other things that I am too big for now, too. I am too big to eat baby food and play with baby toys, and I am too big to take naps all the time like I did when I was little. I'm glad that I am growing up! I can ride a bike and eat pizza and play with toys that are lots more fun than baby toys!

What fun things can you do now that you couldn't do when you were little?

And now I am big enough to be in school, and I am glad! I'm learning about reading and writing and math! And I am also learning about responsibilities. **Do you know what responsibilities are?** Responsibilities are jobs that we have to do when we are old enough to do them. **What are your responsibilities, now that you are older?** I have chores to do at home, and I have responsibilities at school, too, just like you do. When we are in school, rules remind us to pay attention to our teacher and follow directions, and take turns, and be nice to each other so that all of us have a chance to learn!

And there are rules and responsibilities at home, too. **What rules do you follow at home?** Rules at home help keep us safe and healthy!

I wrote a poem to help me remember to follow the rules at school. I hope it helps you, too. When you follow the rules, be proud of yourself, and say to yourself, **"Good for Me!"**

Draw a picture of yourself following the rules on page 54.

I'm Not as Young as I Used to Be

**I'm not as young as I used to be
When I was one or two or three.**

**I follow the rules, because you see,
That is my responsibility.**

When I'm in the classroom my job is to learn.
I listen to others and wait for my turn.

I pay attention and concentrate,
And I follow directions right away.

I don't bother others. They're learning, too.
I'm quiet and helpful. There's schoolwork to do!

I do my best work all the day through.
Listening and learning is my job to do.

Because . . .

**I'm not as young as I used to be
When I was one or two or three.**

**I follow the rules, because you see,
That is my responsibility!**

This is me following the rules.

Parent's Guide to . . . GOOD THINKING

The Reason for This Lesson

One of the most important jobs we have as parents is to keep children safe from harm. You can't be with him to protect him all the time, so you need to teach him about the things in his world that could be dangerous to him and encourage him to use **"Good Thinking!"** Children who act first and think later (like Bouncer) may need extra help to stay out of danger!

The Story Bouncer has learned about some of the dangerous things in his world, and has written a rap about using **"Good Thinking"** to help other children stay safe!

Getting the Most from This Lesson

Talk about safety at home and at school.

As your child goes out into the world, he will need to be able to "Take a look around" and identify things that could hurt him. Some things to talk about:

- At home

  Stay away from hot stoves and ovens
  Watch out for slippery wet floors
  Keep electrical appliances away from water
  Never help yourself to medicine or vitamins!
  Keep toys picked up so you don't trip over them!
  Have an escape route in case of fire
  Know how to make an emergency phone call
  Don't ever let strangers in
  Know who to call if you are scared!

- Outside

  Don't talk to strangers
  Know your address and phone number
  Stay on the sidewalk whenever possible
  Always wait for the green light
  Never play your radio too loud
  Never try to play with a strange dog
  Never run in parking lots
  Hold hands!

- Around other kids

  Know right from wrong and do the right thing!

- At school

  Playground safety
  Sidewalk safety
  Staying with the class
  Never leaving the classroom without permission!
  Walking in classrooms and hallways
  Scissor and pencil safety
  Fire drill procedures
  And so on!

Other Fun Things to Do

- Make a game out of identifying dangerous things. Start with, **"Take a look around and tell me what do you see? I see something out there that could hurt you and me!"** Let your child point out dangerous things to you and talk about what makes them dangerous. And consistently let your child know how proud you are of him when he does his chores and follows the rules!

Be proud of your child when he can identify dangerous things and avoid them. It could save his life someday!

Bouncer raps about . . . GOOD THINKING

I've written a rap for you today.
It's about living and learning to be safe always!

Take a look around and tell me, what do you see?
There are lots of things out there that can hurt you and me!

Know what they are and know what to do,
And use good thinking! It will get you through!

When you're at home or you're at school,
Learn to follow the good thinking rules.

> *Good thinking!*
> *Use good thinking,*
> *And you will be*
> *smart like me!*

> *Good thinking!*
> *Use good thinking,*
> *Or you're living*
> *too dangerously!*

Stop, look, and listen when you travel
    around.
Pay attention out there and listen to the
    sounds.

When your radio's loud, the sound fills
    your ears.

And when cars are around, you need your
    ears to hear!

Remember cars are big and you are small,
And sometimes they can't even see you at
    all.

So it's up to you
to look out for them,
So stop, look, and listen
and your fun won't end!

> *Good thinking!*
> *Use good thinking,*
> *And you will be*
> *smart like me!*
>
> *Good thinking!*
> *Use good thinking,*
> *Or you're living*
> *too dangerously!*

Things at home can cause trouble for you.
Know what they are and know what to do!

Things that are hot can hurt you a lot,
So be careful in the kitchen! Stay away
    from hot pots!

Medicines and pills are things that can
    kill.
Don't ever help yourself or you'll be very
    ill!

If you're home alone, don't let strangers
    know.
And if you get scared, you'd better know
    where to go!

> *Good thinking! Use good thinking,*
> *And you will be smart like me!*
>
> *Good thinking! Use good thinking,*
> *Or you're living too dangerously!*

There are kids out there who are not your
   friends.
They want to get you in trouble, but don't
   let them!

They want to play with fire because they
   say it's cool.
You know better than that! You learned it
   in school.

When they see a gun, they might want to
   play.
But you know the right thing is to get
   away.

They smoke and drink and they tell you to
   try it.
You're too smart for that! You're not going
   to buy it!

> **Good thinking!**
> **Use good thinking,**
> **And you will be**
> **smart like me!**
>
> **Good thinking!**
> **Use good thinking,**
> **Or you're living**
> **too dangerously!**

When you're using your good thinking
For all the world to see,
Be proud of yourself, and say,
"Good for Me!"

Now just turn the page and find the
   place for you
To draw a picture of good thinking
   and knowing what to do!

This is me using good thinking!

Parent's Guide to . . . DOING THE RIGHT THING

The Reason for This Lesson

Even though we do our best to teach our children right from wrong, there will always be people around who make it seem more fun to be "bad" than to be "good." Those are the times when your child will need some extra encouragement from inside himself to do the right thing, even when there is "no one to see."

The Story Bouncer goes to the store with some kids who steal candy and encourage him to do the same. He is proud of himself when he does the right thing, and learns that real friends are kids who help him be his best self.

Getting the Most from This Lesson

Has anyone ever tried to talk your child into doing the wrong thing?

All children know kids who think it's more fun to be bad than to be good. They know bullies and kids who lie and cheat. Talk about them and about doing the right thing!

Who are your child's good friends?

Children also know kids who play fair, share, and who want to do the right thing. Talk about them and encourage your child to spend time with them. Be sure to let your child know that his good friends bring out the best in him and help him do things that he can be proud of.

Other Fun Things to Do

- Take the time when reading stories or talking about TV programs to talk about the characters who are doing the right thing and those doing the wrong thing. Sometimes it's not easy to do the right thing!

- You may be using "thumbs up" (or another signal) and a smile to acknowledge your child's good deeds. Develop a signal (maybe "thumbs down") to use when you see someone or read about a bad deed. Remember that your child really does want to learn the difference between right and wrong things.

- Cut and paste pictures from magazines or draw pictures showing people doing the right thing. Then you might do the same to illustrate people doing the wrong thing.

- Take photos of your child doing chores, following the rules, being a good friend, and doing the right thing! Display them proudly!

When your child does the right thing, even when there is "no one to see," reward your honest and trustworthy youngster with your highest praise!

Boucer talks about . . . DOING THE RIGHT THING

9

Last week, some kids I know wanted me to go to the store with them. When we got there, they told me that it would be easy to steal candy from the store because there was no one around to see us. They took some candy and put it in their pocket and didn't pay for it, and they told me to take some, too. I wanted the kids to be my friends, but I also wanted to do the right thing, and I know that stealing is wrong!

Has anyone ever tried to talk you into doing the wrong thing? What did you do? I know that stealing is wrong, so I didn't take any candy that day. And I was proud of myself for making the right choice and doing the right thing! But those kids won't be my friends anymore.

And there are some other kids who don't want to share with me or to take turns playing games. They want their way all the time. Sometimes they hurt me, and once they broke one of my toys on purpose. And they said that they wouldn't be my friend if I didn't let them have their way. **Do you know people like that?**

I don't play with people like that anymore. People who want to get you in trouble are not your friends, no matter what they say!

Now I play with people who want to do the right thing, just like me. And I have lots more fun than before! And I learned that **real** friends are people who want to help you be your very best self, like my friends in the *"Good for Me!"* Club.

We take turns when we play and sometimes we share our toys. And we would never steal or hurt something that belongs to someone else! But the most important thing is telling the truth. We never tell lies to each other. And when we have problems to work out, we don't fight about them. We share and take turns. That's the right thing to do!

Now that we are getting older, our parents aren't with us all the time to help us do the right thing. Having good friends to be with makes it easy to do the right thing, have fun, and be proud of ourselves. **Do you have friends who help you do the right thing?**

I wrote a poem to help me remember to do the right thing. When you do the right thing, be proud of yourself, and say to yourself, **"Good for Me!"**

Draw a picture of a time when you did the right thing, even when there was no one to see, on page 66.

64

What Do You Do When There's No One to See?

What do you do when there's no one to see?
Do you take things,
or break things,
or hurt property?

NO WAY!

I know right from wrong, and I choose the right way.
And I'm proud of myself when I do the right thing!

What do you do when you want your way?
Is cheating,
or teasing,
or fighting okay?

NO WAY!

I know right from wrong, and I choose the right way.
And I'm proud of myself when I do the right thing!

What do you do when you make a mistake?
Do you lie,
or hide it,
or give others the blame?

NO WAY!

I know right from wrong, and I choose the right way.
And I'm proud of myself when I do the right thing!

This is me doing the right thing.

Snuggles learns about . . .

FEELING GOOD

BEING HAPPY

The Reason for This Lesson

When someone smiles at you, it's hard not to smile back! And you want your child to get lots of smiles from others! So, the more he smiles, the better. (And have you ever noticed that it's not possible to have an "attitude problem" and smile at the same time!)

Also, it's really important for your child to learn about his special talents and share them with others. (This is an excellent way to have fun without the TV set!) Because the more you share your talents with others, the more smiles you get. And the more smiles you get, the happier you are. And the happier you are, the more you want to share with others. And the more you share with others, the more you smile. And the more you smile, the more smiles you get back. And the more smiles you get back, the better!

The Story Snuggles shares that he was named "Snuggles" because he loves to snuggle up with his favorite people and toys. Snuggling makes him feel happy inside, and he loves to show it! Discovering his special talents and sharing them with others makes him feel happy, too.

Getting the Most from This Lesson

What are your child's favorite things to snuggle?
Make sure your child has lots of things to snuggle! This is a stress management skill that can also come in handy later in life!

How does your child show it when he is happy?
When your child is happy, be sure to tell him that you love his smile and his twinkly eyes!

**What is your child really good at
and how does he share his special
talents with others?**

All children are really good at something! (Running, reading, counting, coloring, cutting, pasting, telling stories, singing, dancing . . .) Make sure that your child knows that he has special talents and encourage him to share his gifts with others. Show your pride in him by displaying his work, having talent shows, and watching him play!

Other Fun Things to Do

- Do frequent Snuggles "Smile Checks." (Freeze and check your smile in the nearest mirror!)

- Take photos of your child showing how he looks when he is happy (make sure his eyes are twinkly!). You might want to start with, "When I'm happy deep inside, you will surely know it. You can see it right away! This is how I show it!" Then take the photo!

- You can make your own Snugglies out of socks and fiber fill. Use permanent markers to make facial features and hair (or use yarn). Stitch closed so the fiber fill won't come out. Sprinkle them with pixie dust (fine glitter or baby powder) so that every time they are snuggled, they make happy thoughts!

- Make and decorate paper "frames" to display and save your child's art work. Make a frame out of a manila envelope or two pieces of construction paper taped together. Just cut an opening for the front and leave the top open to slide papers in and out. To be extra fancy, you could put a piece of clear plastic inside to simulate glass. Decorate and display with pride!

Encourage smiles, twinkly eyes, and expressions of your child's budding talents whenever you can!

Snuggles talks about . . . ## BEING HAPPY

Can you guess how I got my name? People call me Snuggles because I like to snuggle up with the people I love. When you snuggle, you get close and hug. Sometimes you can rock back and forth when you snuggle, just like rocking a baby. I like to snuggle with my pets and my favorite toys, too. **Do you have a favorite toy that you like to snuggle?**

Did you know that everyone needs to snuggle? Some doctors think that we need to snuggle every day to stay healthy and happy!

I have learned that when I feel sad or lonely, snuggling my favorite toy helps me feel better and feel happy again.

When I start feeling happy again, the good feelings start inside me and push their way out. Then you can see the happy all over me! My face has a smile, my eyes are twinkly, and my tail wags! I'll bet you do the same thing when you are happy—except for wagging a tail, of course!

How do you show it when you are happy?

When I am happy, I feel special, and I think about the things that make me special. I think about the things that I can do really well. All of us have something special that we are good at. Those special things are called "gifts" or "talents." Now that you're growing up, it is important to find all the special gifts or talents you have! **What special things do you do really well?** I am good at drawing, and when I draw, I feel happy inside.

There is one other thing about being happy. When you share your talents with other people, your happy feelings grow even bigger! And theirs do, too! **How do you share your talents with other people?** I like to draw pictures for people. And when people smile, I know that I have used my special talent to make them happy, too! That really feels good!

I wrote a poem about the different things people do when they are happy. When you are happy and doing the things that you do best, be proud of yourself and say to yourself, **"Good for Me!"**

Draw a picture of your special talent on page 74.

My Eyes Have a Twinkle

When I'm happy deep inside, you will surely know it.
You can see it right away! This is how I show it!

There's a twinkle in my eyes, and on my face a smile,
And a special glow from deep inside that shines at least a mile!

And when you see me glow that way, I'm happy as can be,
Because I'm using special gifts that were given just to me.

My hands were made to draw and paint,
and my feet were made to dance,
And my voice just loves to sing out loud
Whenever I get a chance!

Sometimes I like to ride my bike
or to skate along a path,
And race against the summer wind—
I love to go so fast!

Sometimes I use more quiet gifts,
and find the place within me,
To take good care of the things I love,
and snuggle them so near me.

And then I'm truly feeling good, I'm happy and I'm glowing.
And when I give to those I love, my glow is overflowing!

We all are given special gifts to share with one another,
You, too, can find your special glow that is not like any others.

Your gifts belong to you alone, no one can take them from you,
And when you find them deep inside, share them with folks who love
you!

This is my special talent.

THE MOST SPECIAL FEELING

The Reason for This Lesson

Love is the most special feeling. If we're lucky, we learn about love early in life and we are surrounded by people who affirm it every day. We all want our children to feel loved and safe and valued.

And we want to protect them from the pain that comes from losing or being separated from a loved one, but that's not so easy. In today's ever-changing world, children are often separated from people that they love. Children miss their parents when they start school. When families move due to job changes, children miss the people they were close to. And sometimes parents separate or divorce.

More than ever, today's children need to find ways of continuing to love while coping with their losses. And the lessons they learn about the most special feeling will serve them well as their lives and loves continue.

The Story   Snuggles learns about the power of love when his grandmother moves away. He learns that love can make you very happy or very sad. He also learns that someone's love for you can be felt anytime, and you can send your love to them whenever you feel it. He also learns that the U.S. Mail can help you send your love!

Getting the Most from This Lesson

Does your child have loved ones far away?

Talk about the people your child misses and let him know that the sadness he feels is because he cares for the people he misses.

What things remind your child of the people he loves?

Photographs and mementos of special times your child has spent can remind him of the people he loves. Keeping those things close can help when he really misses his loved ones.

How does your child send love to people he misses?

Help your child write letters or draw special pictures for people he misses who are far away. When he is at school, and you are not there with him, let him know that he can send you his love anytime!

Other Fun Things to Do

- Have a regular time when you and your child think about someone you love and make something special for them to show your love.

- Sometimes children forget what special faces look like, and that can be a very frightening experience. Make sure your child has photos of you and other people that he loves.

- **Send Valentines anytime!** (Maybe on the 14th of every month!)

- Children often love and miss their pets, too. Talk about them, draw pictures of them, and make special things for them, too!

Have you hugged your child today and told him how much you love him? Good for you!

Snuggles talks about... THE MOST SPECIAL FEELING

Last week, my grandmother moved far away, and I really miss her. I cried a lot when she left. And sometimes when I am away from other people in my family, I miss them, too, and it makes me sad not to be with them. Sometimes I even feel sad when I'm away from my pets. Sometimes I miss them the most when I am at school. **Do you ever feel sad when you're away from people you care about?**

Before my grandmother moved away, she told me about a special feeling, the most special feeling of all. It's a feeling that makes you feel warm and snuggly and happy inside. Love is always with you and God is always with you, too. And when you feel these things, it's the happiest that you can be. And when you feel it, you are the luckiest person in the whole world.

Do you know what the most special feeling is?

It's love! Love is the most special feeling. But when you love someone and you can't be with them, you miss them. And that's the saddest that you can be.

My grandmother told me that love is special because it never goes away like other things do. She said that the love she has for me is always with me, and when I want to feel her love, all I have to do is think about her. She gave me a picture of us together so I can remember a special time we had. I have other things in my room that remind me of her, too. **Do you have things that remind you of the people you love?**

She knew that I would miss her, so she told me that the best thing to do when you miss someone is to send love to them. I send love to her in letters and pictures and in special thoughts. And she sends love back to me.

She told me one more special thing about love. She said that there is **always** room in your heart for more love, no matter how much is already there. And that the more love you give to others, the more you get back. Now I try to send love to everyone special to me. **How do you send love to people who are special to you?**

I wrote a poem to help me remember what love feels like. I hope it helps you remember, too. When you have learned what love feels like, be proud of yourself and say to yourself, **"Good for Me!"**

Draw a picture of the special people you love on page 80.

What Starts in Your Heart?

Here is a riddle for you today.
I hope you can guess it right away!

What starts in your heart and warms you inside?
Is it hot chocolate?
No, but that's a good try!

What makes you want to be near
And snuggle real close?
Is it a warm blanket?
Good guess, but no.

What makes you feel happy
From your head to your toes?
Let me guess now!
I'm sure that I know!

It has to be love!
Am I right this time?
Love is warm and snuggly
And happy inside!

You've solved the riddle.
I'm proud of you!
Love is always the answer
That will see you through!

Now there's just one more thing that I want to say,
To be really happy, you need love each day!

These are the people that I love.

FEELING BETTER

The Reason for This Lesson

Everyone has bad days sometimes. It's important to learn how to get through them, how to feel better, and not give up hope for the future. Some kids, like Snuggles, seem to have more than their share of unhappy times. To get through these times, it's important to know that all feelings come and go (the bad ones and the good ones), and that when you are feeling sad, you are not powerless. There are things that you can do to feel better.

It's really important for children to learn how to comfort themselves when their loved ones are not around. Special objects (especially snuggly ones) help them feel secure and safe during lonely times. Pictures of people they love can also bring them comfort. All of us could benefit from having a quiet place in our homes where we feel safe and can feel God's love for us.

The Story   Snuggles has a bad week, but he has learned that bad feelings don't last forever. He has also learned that some of the things he has in his room can give him comfort, and that he can use his imagination to go to a special place in his mind (his "Cozy Corner") where he feels safe and loved.

Getting the Most from This Lesson

Have you and your child ever had a bad day?

Share some of the things that have gone wrong in your day. Laugh about some of them if you can! Even though you might have felt terrible when bad things were happening, those bad feelings never last forever (thank heaven!).

What special things does your child have that help him feel safe and loved when you're not with him?

Ask your child about the special things that bring him comfort and keep them nearby.

Have your child imagine a special place where he feels safe and loved.

During a peaceful time, ask your child to close his eyes and imagine a very special place that was made just for him. It's a happy place where he feels safe. When he gets to his special place, ask him to remember as much as he can about it. What does it look like? Are there animals there? Are there people there? (Remember it's his place! It could even be on another planet!) Talk about his special place and draw pictures of it.

These wonderful places can be a part of your child's "Cozy Corner" and can help him feel peaceful and safe whenever he thinks of them. (This is a good stress management exercise for you to do, too!)

Other Fun Things to Do

• Make a **Cozy Corner** in your child's room.

Decorate a special place near your child's bed with big white clouds or beautiful rainbows—**anything** that makes your child feel safe and loved. And keep special photos and mementos nearby. And don't forget special snuggly things!

When it's time to go to sleep, you and your child can enjoy this peaceful place together, and he can travel to the "Cozy Corner" in his imagination.

When your child can comfort himself during unhappy times, be proud of him.

Snuggles talks about . . . **FEELING BETTER**

I feel better now, but last week was really terrible! The kid that picks on me said mean things to me and called me names, I had a fight with my best friend, someone stole my lunch box, I ripped my favorite shirt, I lost my homework, and I got in trouble at home. **Have you ever had a terrible week?**

Sometimes when I have weeks like that, I feel all alone and sad, and sometimes I want to give up. But I have learned some things about feeling better that you might already know.

I learned that unhappy feelings don't last forever. Our feelings come and go. I remember that terrible week, but I don't feel bad anymore! Those feelings are gone now, and I'm glad!

I also learned that there are special places I can go that help me feel better when I feel sad. I have a special place in my room that I call my Cozy Corner. I keep things there that remind me of happy times and of being safe and loved. There are pictures of people that I love, a special blanket that I snuggle, a special rock that reminds me of a happy day, and a special book to read. Some people keep a Bible there to remind them that God is always with them. **What things would you put in your Cozy Corner?**

When I am in my Cozy Corner I imagine being in a place where I feel safe and loved, like my grandmother's house, my friend's house, or under a special tree. Sometimes I imagine being on a cloud floating up to the sky! **Can you imagine a place where you feel safe and loved?**

When I am in my Cozy Corner, I feel better. And I go there every night before I go to sleep because I have good dreams when I am in my Cozy Corner!

I wrote a poem about my Cozy Corner. When you know how to feel better when you are sad, be proud of yourself, and say to yourself, **"Good for Me!"**

Draw a picture of your Cozy Corner on page 86.

My Cozy Corner

I have a Cozy Corner that belongs to only me.
I go there when I'm feeling sad and need some comforting.

It's a peaceful place that's mine alone. I've made it just that way.
It's in my imagination, and it's only a thought away.

I go there when I'm feeling sad,
And I tell myself, "Remember,
Be patient now, and you will see,
You won't feel this way forever."

And I find my Cozy Corner and I snuggle up real tight.
And soon I'm feeling peaceful, and everything's all right.

And when I'm hurt or lonely
I can go there, too.
And I tell myself, "Remember,
You won't always feel so blue."

And I find my Cozy Corner, and I snuggle up real tight.
And soon I'm feeling peaceful, and everything's all right.

And when I'm feeling all alone
And things are dark and scary,
I tell myself, "Remember now,
You won't always feel so wary."

And I find my Cozy Corner, and I snuggle up real tight.
And soon I'm feeling peaceful, and everything's all right.

This is my Cozy Corner.

Parent's Guide to . . . **SAYING "NO"**

The Reason for This Lesson

Although it's sometimes hard to believe, lots of children can't wait to grow up! Children who are unhappy seem to want to grow up the fastest. And when children think about being grown up, they think about being able to do the things that only adults are allowed to do, like smoke cigarettes and drink. And sadly, many children also see adults using drugs and doing other illegal things that seem like "fun."

It's important for children to be able to visualize themselves as happy adults, and to understand that healthy, happy adults choose not to smoke, drink, use drugs, or participate in illegal activities because those things are unhealthy and wrong.

The Story   Snuggles can't wait to grow up and be happy and do what he wants to do. He is encouraged by an older child to smoke a cigarette because it is "fun" and it is what grown-ups do. Snuggles is tempted, but remembers the person that he wants to be when he grows up. He knows that smoking isn't a part of his dream and he says, "No!"

Getting the Most from This Lesson

Does your child know kids who do things they're not supposed to do?

Talk about those kids and why what they are doing is wrong. Let your child know that you know people who do the wrong thing, too, but that you don't want to be like them.

**Have other kids ever encouraged
your child to do the wrong thing?
What happened?**

Older children often try to talk younger ones into sharing their secret "fun." If your child said, "No!" let him know how proud you are of him. If he tried something wrong, let him know how glad you are that he told you and talk about doing the right thing next time.

Other Fun Things to Do

• Talk about the future and all the things your child might want to do when he grows up. Write and illustrate stories together. Making healthy choices and saying, "No!" to things that might hurt him will help him achieve his goals.

• Talk about heroes on television, in your family, or in the Bible. Which ones said "no" to things that would hurt them? Which ones gave in to temptation? You can also talk about the consequences of illegal activities. Characters who do illegal things on television might not go to jail, but in the real world, they certainly would!

There are lots of temptations out there! Continue to reward your child for resisting them and let him know that you are proud of him!

Snuggles talks about. . . SAYING "NO"

Sometimes I can't wait to grow up and be happy! I have lots of dreams about how I want my life to be. I want to finish school, and have a good job, and live where I want to. And someday I want to have a family, too. And I want to be grown up because then nobody will tell me when to go to bed or when to clean my room! And nobody will yell at me when I'm grown up. Sometimes I just can't wait to grow up!

When I see big kids around, they look like they are having lots of fun, and they look grown up. But some of them do things that are against the law and can hurt them.

Some smoke cigarettes. Some kids steal things. Some drink beer. And I even heard about some kids who use drugs.

Do you know kids who do things they are not supposed to do?

One time, one of those kids tried to give me a cigarette and told me that I would be grown up if I learned to smoke. **Has that ever happened to you? What did you do?** I said "No, thank you!" because I know that smoking won't make me more grown up. The only thing that can make me more grown up is lots more birthdays!

I know that I will have to wait to grow up, just like you. And when I grow up I want to be happy, and I want to be proud of myself. I have lots of dreams about the life that is ahead of me. And when I think about my dreams, I want them to come true. So I say, "No!" to things that would hurt me.

I wrote a poem to help me remember that. I hope it helps you, too. When you can do the right thing while you are waiting to grow up, be proud of yourself, and say to yourself, **"Good for Me!"**

Draw a picture of the things you want to do when you grow up on page 92.

Close Your Eyes
and See with Your Heart

Sometimes when I feel lonely,
Some big kids come around.
They say to come along with them,
And I won't feel so down.

They say they'll be my best friends,
And teach me to be cool.
They say they'll teach me secret things
That we don't learn in school.

But inside my heart is a feeling
That tells me not to go,
But if I say no, they won't be my friends,
And I'll be all alone.

**Then I close my eyes and see with my heart
All the things I want to be.
And then I say "No!" to the kids that are wrong,
And I say to myself, "Good for Me!"**

I remember the me that I want to be
And the path that I will take,
And I'm proud of myself when I say, "No!"
Those bad kids should go jump in a lake!

**Then I close my eyes and see with my heart
All the things I want to be.
And then I say "No!" to the kids that are wrong,
And I say to myself, "Good for Me!"**

This is who I want to be when I grow up.

Spot learns about . . .

DOING GOOD

"MAGIC" WORDS

The Reason for This Lesson

(We know that words by themselves hold no power, but generations of children have been taught that the "magic words" to use with others are "please and thank you." This lesson continues that tradition.)

One of the biggest concerns parents have is the growing number of children who appear to have "attitude problems." Children who are often otherwise delightful and well behaved tend to be rude, demanding, disrespectful, and generally lacking in "social graces."

While it's true that children are born "narcissistic" and see themselves as the center of their world, they are not born rude and disrespectful. Those behaviors are learned along the way. It seems that children see examples of rudeness being rewarded, then they try it to see what happens. Many parents, convinced by "experts" that they should ignore and not punish inappropriate behavior, try to pretend that the rudeness did not take place and proceed to grant children's requests. (Think for a moment about what would have happened to you if you had behaved rudely as a child! You can be sure that yesterday's parents did **not** ignore disrespectful behavior!)

And with today's lifestyle being more casual than yesterday's, far fewer opportunities present themselves for children to learn and practice good manners. For example, instead of gathering together at a table for family meals, using "good" dishes (not the jelly jars), inquiring about everyone's day, and asking politely if someone would "please, pass the salt," many of us now sit around a television set and compete with one another for the biggest piece of pizza out of a cardboard box!

At any rate, children who use good manners and show appreciation for the help they receive are much more likely to have good experiences in the world than children with "attitude problems!" And we can help them by adding this piece to their "ideal child" puzzle!

The Story Spot sees a magician make wonderful things happen by using "magic" words. He thinks about how the "magic" words he knows (**"please"** and **"thank you"**) also make good things happen!

Getting the Most from This Lesson

What are "magic" words?
Be sure to use "please" and "thank you" often!

What things does your child need help with?
By talking about the things that your child needs help with, you can let him know that those are good times to use "magic" words.

Other Fun Things to Do

- Make a game of counting the number of times you hear others use **"please"** and **"thank you."** You might want to do the same thing with TV shows. (How polite **are** children's favorite TV characters?) Or play a version of "Simon Says" using "magic" words!

- Once you have mastered "magic" words, include more advanced lessons on the use of "excuse me," "pardon me," formal introductions, telephone etiquette, movie theater etiquette, and formal dining (complete with tablecloths and flowers!).

- Make a supply of "Thank you" notes to be used to acknowledge gifts and favors.

Yours can be a kinder, more polite home. You can start by using "magic" words!

Spot talks about . . . **"MAGIC" WORDS**

Last week I saw a real magician! He made rabbits come out of hats, and he made people float on air! And before he did every one of his tricks, he said a magic word. It was wonderful! When I watched the show, someone told me that the magic words made all those wonderful things happen, but I know that's not true. People can do magic tricks without using any words at all!

But then I started thinking about magic words, and I wondered if there were any special words that make wonderful things happen when you use them. Right away, I thought of some! **Do you know what they are?**

The magic words are, **"Please,"** and **"Thank you,"** and I learned how they work! You can use them, too!

Every single day there are things that you would like other people to do for you. You might need some help with your work. You might want to borrow a toy. You might want an extra helping at dinner time. Or you might want someone to give you a hug! **Can you think of other things that you want people to do for you?**

When you use "magic" words when you ask for things, it shows that you care about the people who help you, and it shows them that you appreciate the things that they do for you. If you want to make wonderful things happen, just use "magic" words every day!

I wrote a poem to help me remember how important it is to say, "Please," and, "Thank you," when someone does something nice for me. When you can use these "magic" words every day, be proud of yourself, and say to yourself, **"Good for Me!"**

Please draw a picture of yourself using "magic" words on page 100. Thank you very much.

Some Words
Are "Magic"

Some words are "magic" because when they're used,
They make good things happen for me and for you.

Just a few "magic" words can show that you care
And appreciate it when others share.

**"Please" and "Thank you," it's plain to see,
Have "magic" powers for you and for me!**

**When you have a request, add some "magic" to it.
"Please" is the very best word to do it!**

**Saying "Thank you" is "magic" (and the right thing to do!)
When somebody does something nice for you!**

Use these few "magic" words and I'm sure you will see,
That your world is a much nicer place to be!

This is me using "magic" words.

Parent's Guide to . . . **BEING SORRY**

The Reason for This Lesson

Everyone makes mistakes and **nobody** wants to be in trouble! The hard thing to do is to take responsibility for the mistakes we make, apologize, and try to correct them. And ideally, we learn from them and become more successful in the future.

We all know that "Honesty is the best policy," but most of us would like to avoid the unpleasant consequences of admitting our mistakes. The unpleasant feelings of guilt and fear are things that we would wish to avoid if we could! And it's the desire to avoid these feelings that makes us want to make as few mistakes as possible. So the next time we're in a hurry, or tempted to say something to hurt someone's feelings, we remember what might happen as a result, and we make better choices.

The Story Spot was in a hurry and spilled milk all over the floor. He was tempted to do the wrong thing and blame someone else, but he took responsibility for his mistake, apologized, and cleaned up his mess. He also promised to be more careful next time!

Getting the Most from This Lesson

What kind of mistakes happen at home and at school?

Talk about the usual mistakes that happen when we are in a hurry or when we are not being careful. Also talk about the kind of mistakes that hurt people's feelings!

What should you do when you make a mistake?

You can help your child learn to say he is sorry, to try to make things right, and to try to do better in the future.

Other Fun Things to Do

- See mistakes as opportunities for creative problem solving. If there are consistent problems (spilling things, breaking things, etc.), take time to talk about how to avoid the problem in the future. It may mean rearranging things or having certain places off-limits . . . . Work with your child to find a solution!

- When characters in stories make mistakes, take a minute to discuss how they might make amends and what they can do later to avoid the same mistake.

When your child admits his mistakes and makes efforts to correct them, let him know you are proud of him!

102

Spot talks about . . . **BEING SORRY**

What a week I had last week! It seemed like I couldn't do anything right! I broke one of my mom's favorite picture frames because I was running around in the house, I got angry with my best friend and I said things that hurt his feelings, and this morning I spilled milk all over the floor because I was in too much of a hurry. **Have you ever done things like that?**

I felt sorry after I did those things, but I didn't know what to do to make it better. And I didn't want to get in trouble. Nobody likes being in trouble! So when my mom asked me about the milk, I thought about blaming it on my brother because he was in the kitchen, too. But I knew that wasn't the right thing to do, so I didn't blame it on him!

When I feel sorry because of something I have done, I wish I could start over again and take back what I did or what I said. But I can't do that so I have to find another way to make it better. **Do you know what to do when you feel sorry for something you have done?**

The right thing to do is to start by making an apology. When you make an apology, you say that you are sorry and try to make things better, like cleaning up a mess you made. Then you should promise from your heart to try to do better next time.

When you've made a mistake or hurt someone's feelings, an apology is the best way to start to make things better! And you should **never** blame someone else and get them in trouble for a mistake you make.

I wrote a poem to help me remember to apologize when I make a mistake. I hope it helps you remember, too. When you know how to apologize when you feel sorry for something you have done, be proud of yourself and say to yourself, **"Good for Me!"**

Draw a picture of yourself saying you are sorry for a mistake you made on page 106.

Oops!

Oops! I made a mistake!
I didn't mean to do it.

I'll really try to do better next time.
I'm sorry, and I want you to know it.

Oops! I made a mistake!
I'll make an apology.

First I will start with words from my heart,
"I'm sorry. Please, will you excuse me?"

Oops! I hurt your feelings.
I didn't mean to do it.

I'm feeling bad that I made you sad,
And I really want you to know it.

Oops! I hurt your feelings.
I'll make an apology.

First I will start with words from my heart,
"I'm sorry. Please, will you forgive me?"

This is me saying I'm sorry for a mistake I made.

Parent's Guide to . . . OUR WORLD

The Reason for This Lesson

As we learn more about our world, we begin to understand that environmental mismanagement in one area can have an impact on the entire planet. But the good news is that as we take action to preserve our neighborhood environment, our actions can benefit the whole world. We all need to learn to be good stewards of God's creation.

The Story   Spot sees a picture of the earth taken from space and notices that there are no boundaries. There are no lines to separate one country from another or one state from another. He concludes that we share the earth with all other people and living things, and that what we do affects the entire world. He has heard about pollution in the world and the destruction of animal habitats, and he wants to do something to help. He learns that he can help by recycling, reusing, and reducing his needs for more things. He wants to learn more about making the world a better place.

Getting the Most from This Lesson

What can you do to make the world a better place?

Share with your child the things that your family does to make the world a better place (charitable contributions, recycling, etc.).

This is also a good time to talk about the different jobs family members have and how each contributes to making the world a better place.

Other Fun Things to Do

• Recycle! You could make and/or decorate your own recycling containers.

- Have a toy/clothing exchange and donate the leftovers to a local charity.

- Reuse items when possible. Think about all the things you could do with an item you are about to throw away. This can be a real lesson in creative thinking!

- Learn to repair broken things rather than replacing them. You and your child could learn lots of new things about technology together!

- Get to know and appreciate the wildlife in your area.

- Plant trees and gardens and select the environmentally friendliest products to use.

- House plants can help freshen the air inside your home. Let your child help you care for them.

- Select a familiar business or product to learn about (restaurants, super markets, beverages, cars, toys, etc.). Learn about the materials used, where they come from, how they are disposed of, and the impact the product makes on the environment. Support "environmentally friendly" businesses and products!

---

*You and your child **can** make a difference! There are lots of opportunities to do so!*

Spot talks about . . . OUR WORLD

Have you ever seen a picture of the whole earth? Last week I saw one, and the earth is beautiful! The astronauts have taken pictures of it, and it looks like a blue and white ball with brown spots. When you see the earth like that, the countries and states aren't different colors, like they are on our maps. And there aren't any lines to mark the end of one country and the beginning of another! The earth is for everyone to share.

We share the earth with all of the other people on it, with young and old, with people whose skin is a different color than ours, with people who speak different languages than we do, with people who are rich, and with people who are poor. We also share the earth with the animals. The earth is their home, too!

I heard that the earth is getting dirty because of all the trash we throw away. And the air is getting dirty because of all the cars and factories. And some animals are losing their homes and dying because people are cutting down their homes in the trees.

We need to clean up our earth and take better care of it!

When we are being our very best selves, we love our earth, and know that we should take good care of it. And, we work together to make it a better place. **What do you do to make the world a better place?**

When we are being our very best selves, my friends and I share our things with people who are in need. We try not to waste things, like water and food, and we don't buy things that we don't really want or need. And when we throw things away, we recycle our trash. And of course, we are always kind to the animals because the world is their home, too!

I wrote a poem to help me remember how important our world is. I hope it helps you, too. When you can do things to make our world a better place, be proud of yourself and say to yourself, **"Good for Me!"**

Draw a picture of something you are doing to make the world a better place on page 112.

The World
Is My Home

I wonder what tomorrow will be.
It's up to you and it's up to me.

The world is my home, and I want it to be
A better place for you and for me.

There's work to be done. Let's start right away!
What can we do for our world today?

The world is our home, and I want it to be
A better place for you and for me!

This is me making the world a better place!

Parent's Guide to . . . # THE VERY BEST ME

The Reason for This Lesson

It's not always easy to be your very best self! This lesson gives children encouragement to keep up the good work and be proud of themselves!

The Story Spot talks about how he got his name. (You might think it's because of all his spots, but it's not. It's because he likes to "spot" children being their very best selves!) Spot talks about a visit to school and how he "spotted" lots of children doing the right thing. And he "spotted" Dusty, Bouncer, and Snuggles, too. They have come a long way!

Getting the Most from This Lesson

Talk about Looking Good like Dusty

Talk about all the things your child does to stay healthy and keep himself neat and clean. (Don't forget to talk about washing with soap!)

Talk about Being Good like Bouncer

Talk about how much your child has grown, and how proud you are of him when he uses "good thinking" and does the right thing.

Talk about Feeling Good like Snuggles

Talk about your child's special talents and the ways he sends love to others.

113

Talk about Doing Good, like Spot

Tell your child how proud you are of him when he uses magic words and apologizes for his mistakes. And keep working together to make the world a better place!

Other Fun Things to Do

- "Spot" your child being good. You might use small, round stickers ("spots") and give him one each time you see him being his best self. Give him a supply, too, and let him "spot" you!

- As you and your child travel around, have fun "spotting" people being their very best selves like Spot did.

Children can't hear too many times how proud you are of them when you "spot" them being their very best selves!

Spot talks about... THE VERY BEST ME

Can you guess why people call me Spot? You might think it is because of all the spots I wear, but it's not! It's because I like to spot people being their very best selves! When I spot people being their very best selves, it reminds me of how I want to be.

Today on the playground, I spotted lots of people being their very best selves. I saw lots of children playing and taking turns and sharing their toys. They were laughing and having a good time together. They know how to be good friends!

Then as I was walking along, a boy accidentally kicked a ball really hard and it went right over my head! Boy, did I jump! I thought it was going to hit me! But I knew that he didn't kick it at me on purpose. It was an accident.

Then he came up to me to apologize and said that he was sorry. That made me feel better! The right thing to do is to apologize when you make a mistake. It makes people feel better!

When we saw where the ball landed, I knew that he needed help getting it back, and I wanted to help him. But before I could offer to help him, he asked me so politely if I would "please" help him get his ball back. When he used magic words to ask me to help him, he was being his very best self, and I was glad to help him.

And when I gave him his ball back, he thanked me. I could tell that he appreciated my help! Then I wondered what he wanted to be when he grows up . . . maybe he'll play football!

Do you remember how to apologize when you make a mistake? Do you use "magic" words when you ask for help?

Then be proud of yourself! You're being the very best you!

Then I saw my friends being their very best selves!

First I saw Dusty. He was really **Looking Good!** I could tell that he took a bath before school because his hair was neat and clean, and his clothes were clean, too. And when I saw him take time to tie his shoe, I was really proud of him because he was trying to be his very best self!

And I saw him take an apple out of his lunch box. When I first met Dusty, he never ate apples! All he ever wanted to eat were cookies and potato chips!

Then I saw one of Dusty's friends sneeze a big sneeze and cough a big cough. I heard Dusty remind him to cover his sneezes and his coughs and about how germs make people sick. And he told him to be sure to wash his hands with soap to kill the germs. I was really proud of him! When I first met Dusty, he was sick a lot because he didn't take very good care of himself, and he never took time to wash his hands.

Do you remember the things you need to do to Look Good and stay healthy?

If you do, be proud of yourself! You're being the very best you!

117

Then I saw Bouncer playing with some friends. He was really **Being Good!** He was taking turns sharing the swings and being a good friend. And when it was time to line up to go back to the classroom, I could tell that he still wanted to play, but he got in line right away and he didn't push or shove anyone.

Then I saw a boy skip Bouncer in line and step on his foot! I don't like it when people push ahead of me in line, and I know that Bouncer doesn't like it either. I was worried that Bouncer might push him out of line, but he didn't.

I watched Bouncer use his "Bouncer Breathing" to calm down and step back a little. I didn't hear what Bouncer said to the boy who pushed him, but Bouncer stayed calm, and the class went inside. **What do you think Bouncer said to the boy who pushed him?**

When I first met Bouncer, he was in trouble a lot and he sometimes got into fights when someone pushed him or skipped him in line. He's learned to calm down, and follow the rules, and use good thinking, and do the right thing. I'm really proud of him!

Do you remember the things you need to do to Be Good and do the right thing?

If you do, be proud of yourself! You're being the very best you!

118

Then I saw Snuggles carrying a picture that he had made in art class. He has learned that he is really good at making things! One of his pictures is in the office at school where everyone can see it. And he likes to sing, too. He learns new songs so fast and he really has fun singing them! And you should hear some of the great stories he has written. He tells about the neat things his pets do. When I hear his stories, they make me smile!

And I know that the picture he made in art class is for someone he loves who lives far away. He makes lots of things for people he cares about. He even makes special things for his teacher.

When I first met Snuggles, he hardly ever smiled. But today he was smiling and really **Feeling Good.** He has learned about the things he does well, and how to send love to people that he cares about. I'm really proud of him!

Do you remember the things you need to do to Feel Good?

If you do, be proud of yourself! You're being the very best you!

I can Feel Good!

Then I thought about some of the important things I have learned, like being polite and using good manners and apologizing when I make a mistake or hurt someone's feelings.

And I have learned how important it is to take care of the earth we all share. Now I help my family recycle our newspapers and cans and glass containers so they can be used again. And when I outgrow my clothes, I give them to someone who needs them.

And I don't ask for every single toy I see on TV! I have learned to take better care of the things I have so they don't get broken. But if they do break, I am learning how to fix them if I can.

I wrote a poem to help me remember to be the very best me I can be. I hope it helps you, too!

When you can Look Good and Be Good and Feel Good and Do Good, be proud of yourself! You're being the very best you!

Draw a picture of something you do when you are being your very best self on page 122.

The Very Best Me

When I'm sharing and when I'm caring,
I think that you can see,
I'm being the me I was meant to be.
I'm being the very best me!

When I'm a good friend who listens and helps
And keeps good company,
I'm being the friend I was meant to be.
I'm being the very best me!

When I go out of my way to do something nice
For someone who's in need,
And when I'm polite and nice and kind,
I'm being the very best me!

When I do the right thing when I'm all alone
And no one is there to see,
I say to myself, **"Good for Me!"**
I'm being the very best me!

This is me being the very best me!

The Puppies Say . . .
"GOOD-BYE!"

Dusty, Bouncer, Snuggles, and Spot say . . . "**GOOD-BYE!**"

Guess what happened? Our hero, Sparky the Wonder Dog, heard about our **"Good for Me!" Club,** and he came to visit us! He was so proud of us that he wanted to give us a special award. He left one for you, too!

We hope you have had fun with us as we have learned to **Look Good, Be Good, Feel Good,** and **Do Good.**

Always remember to do things you can be proud of every single day. And when you do, say to yourself, **"Good for Me!"**

"Good for Me!"

This award is presented to

_____

Who can **Look Good**
Be Good
Feel Good
and **Do Good**

by _____

Date _____